3

# #HeForShe

S      HE

I AM FOR GENDER EQUALITY
ARE YOU !?

men and women leading the country—but it's not even close. In the highest level of government, just 27 per cent of members of parliament are women. Only one-third of the highest judges in the country are women. Australians recognise the achievements of their fellow citizens with Order of Australia awards—women are nominated for these awards one-third as often as men.

The picture is similar in wider society. Women make up nearly half the workers in Australia and half the university graduates, but 85 per cent of companies are led by men. Men are paid more than women for the same work. Women are more than twice as likely to be sexually harassed at work, usually by men making "inappropriate comments".

Attitudes are harder to describe with statistics. Many people believe that if there are children to raise, it's a woman's job. In the workplace, people tend to see certain jobs—such as police officers, doctors and soldiers—as "belonging" to men. They see other jobs—such as teachers, nurses and cleaners—as women's work.

## About Watson and her speech

Emma Charlotte Duerre Watson was born on 5 April 1990. At nine years of age she auditioned for the role of Hermione Granger in the upcoming *Harry Potter* films. Watson spent the next 10 years acting in eight *Harry Potter* films, while completing primary and high school and starting university. She continues to act, in films and on stage, and has also worked as a fashion model.

In 2014 Watson was appointed a United Nations (UN) Goodwill Ambassador. She uses the position to encourage young women and to promote the United Nations' HeForShe campaign.

The campaign is an example of "positive action". In the past, the struggle for gender equality was by women for women. HeForShe invites men to join the cause, so that everyone benefits. It asks men and boys to speak out and take action against inequalities faced by women and girls. Supporters make a statement and commitment when they sign up: "I am one of billions of men who believe equality for women is a basic human right that benefits us all. And I commit to taking action against gender discrimination and violence in order to build a more just and equal world."

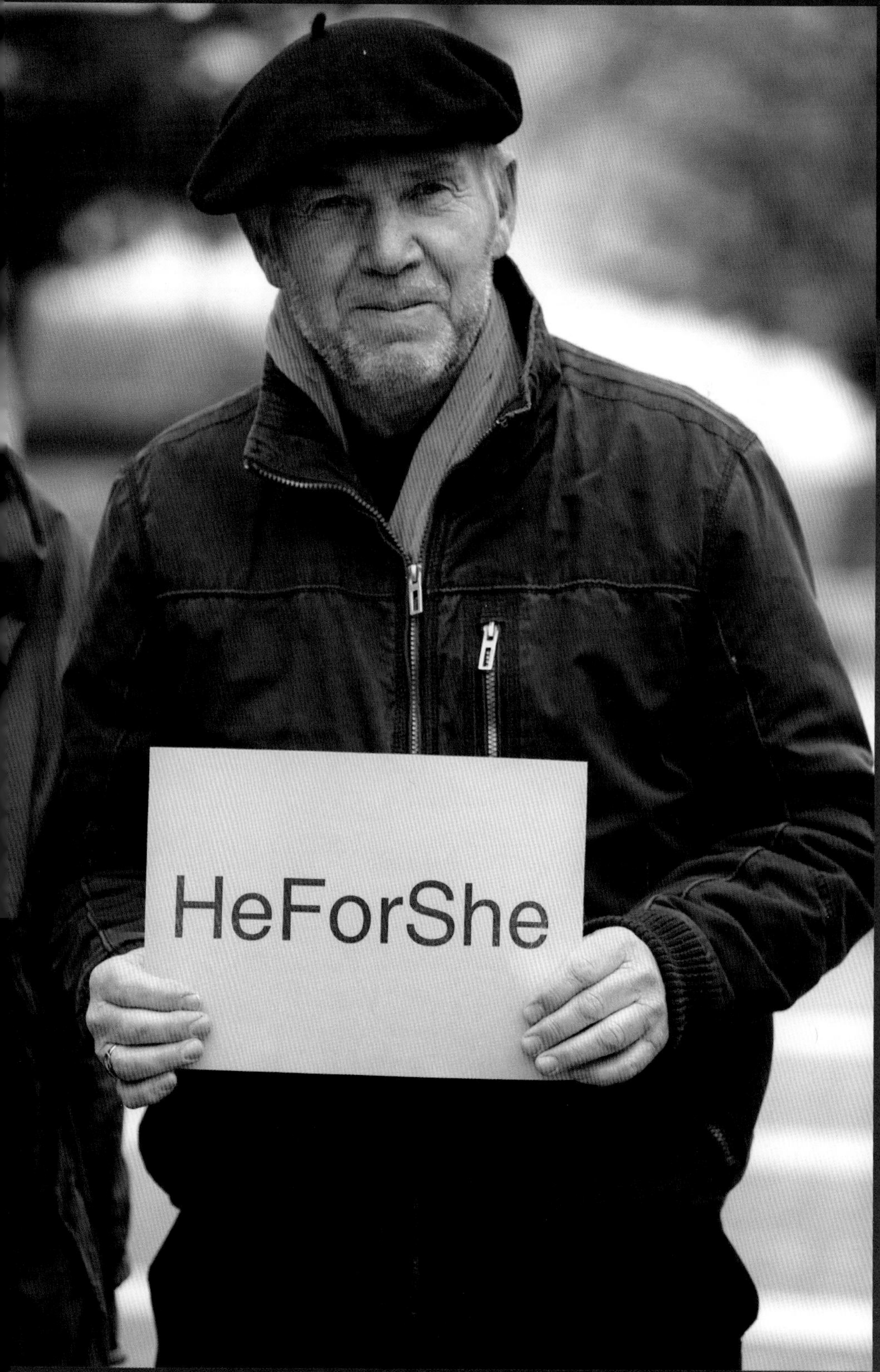
HeForShe

# Emma Watson

Speech at United Nations Headquarters, New York City,
20 September 2014

Your excellencies, UN Secretary-General, President of the
General Assembly, Executive Director of UN Women, and
distinguished guests:

Today we are launching a campaign called HeForShe. I am
reaching out to you because we need your help. We want
to end gender inequality and to do this we need everyone
involved.

This is the first campaign of its kind at the UN. We want to
try and galvanise as many men and boys as possible to be
advocates for change. And we don't just want to talk about
it. We want to try and make sure it's tangible.

I was appointed as Goodwill Ambassador for UN Women
six months ago. The more I spoke about feminism, the
more I realised that fighting for women's rights has too
often become synonymous with man-hating. If there is one
thing I know for certain, it is that this has to stop. For the
record, feminism by definition is the belief that men and
women should have equal rights and opportunities. It is
the theory of political, economic and social equality of the
sexes.

I started questioning gender-based assumptions a long time ago. When I was eight, I was called bossy because I wanted to direct the plays we would put on for our parents. But the boys were not. When at 14, I started to be sexualised by certain elements of the media. At 15, my girlfriends started dropping out of their beloved sports teams because they didn't want to appear muscly. At 18, my male friends were unable to express their feelings.

I decided that I was a feminist and this seemed uncomplicated to me. But my recent research has shown me that feminism has become an unpopular word. Women are choosing not to identify as feminists. Apparently, I am among the ranks of women whose expressions are seen as too strong, too aggressive, isolating and anti-men. Unattractive, even.

Why has the word become such an uncomfortable one? I am from Britain. I think it is right I am paid the same as my male counterparts. I think it is right that I should be able to make decisions about my own body. [Applause] I think it is right that women be involved on my behalf in the policies and the decisions that will affect my life. I think it is right that, socially, I am afforded the same respect as men.

I SUPPORT

 HeForShe

#HeForShe

www.heforshe.org

But sadly, I can say that there is no one country in the world where all women can expect to receive these rights. No country in the world can yet say that they have achieved gender equality. These rights I consider to be human rights but I am one of the lucky ones. My life is a sheer privilege because my parents didn't love me less because I was born a daughter. My school did not limit me because I was a girl. My mentors didn't assume that I would go less far because I might give birth to a child one day. These influences are the gender equality ambassadors who made me who I am today. They may not know it but they are the inadvertent feminists who are changing the world today. We need more of those.

If you still hate the word, it is not the word that is important. It is the idea and the ambition behind it because not all women have received the same rights I have. In fact, statistically, very few have.

In 1997, Hillary Clinton made a famous speech in Beijing about women's rights. Sadly, many of the things that she wanted to change are still true today. But what stood out for me the most was that less than 30 per cent of the audience was male. How can we affect change in the world when only half of it is invited or feel welcomed to participate in the conversation?

he

## Men are invited

Men, I would like to take this opportunity to extend your formal invitation. [Applause] Gender equality is your issue too. Because to date, I've seen my father's role as a parent being valued less by society, despite my needing his presence as a child as much as my mother's. I've seen young men suffering from mental illness, unable to ask for help for fear it would make them less of a man. In fact, in the UK, suicide is the biggest killer of men between 20 and 49, eclipsing road accidents, cancer and coronary heart disease. I've seen men made fragile and insecure by a distorted sense of what constitutes male success. Men don't have the benefits of equality either.

We don't often talk about men being imprisoned by gender stereotypes but I can see that they are. And when they are free, things will change for women as a natural consequence. If men don't have to be aggressive in order to be accepted, women won't feel compelled to be submissive. If men don't have to control, women won't have to be controlled.

Both men and women should feel free to be sensitive. Both men and women should feel free to be strong. It is time that we all perceive gender on a spectrum instead of two sets of opposing ideals. [Applause] If we stop defining each other by what we are not and start defining ourselves by who we are, we can all be freer.

And this is what HeForShe is about. It's about freedom. I want men to take up this mantle so that their daughters, sisters and mothers can be free from prejudice, but also so that their sons have permission to be vulnerable and human too; reclaim those parts of themselves they abandoned; and in doing so be a more true and complete version of themselves.

You might be thinking: Who is this Harry Potter girl [laughter] and what is she doing speaking at the UN? And it's a really good question; I've been asking myself the same thing. All I know is that I care about this problem and I want to make it better. And having seen what I've seen and given the chance, I feel it is my responsibility to say something. Statesman Edmund Burke said, "All that is needed for the forces of evil to triumph is for good men and women to do nothing."

In my nervousness for this speech and in my moments of doubt, I've told myself firmly: If not me, who? If not now, when? If you have similar doubts when opportunities are presented to you, I hope those words will be helpful. Because the reality is if we do nothing, it will take 75 years—or for me to be nearly 100—before women can expect to be paid the same as men for the same work.

Fifteen-point-five million girls will be married in the next 16 years as children. And at current rates, it won't be until 2086 before all rural African girls can have a secondary education.

If you believe in equality, you might be one of those inadvertent feminists that I spoke of earlier, and for this I applaud you. We are struggling for a uniting word but the good news is that we have a uniting movement. It is called HeForShe. I am inviting you to step forward, to be seen and I ask yourself: If not me, who? If not now, when?

Thank you very, very much.

HeForShe

**Emma Watson**
**UN Women Global**
**Goodwill Ambassador**

# Glossary

**advocate**
someone who publicly supports a cause

**affect**
influence

**afforded**
given

**ambassador**
an authorised representative

**audition**
to give a short performance to gain a role in a play, film, etc.

**campaign**
(noun) organised activities to achieve something

**constitutes**
be considered as

**counterpart**
a person with the same role in a different place or organisation

**discrimination**
treating a person or group of people differently, especially in a worse way

**distorted**
changed from the usual form or understanding

**eclipsing**
bigger or more important than something

**fragile**
easily hurt or harmed

**galvanise**
to cause someone to take action

**gender**
male or female

**goodwill**
friendship and favour

**harassed**
upset; tormented

**inadvertent**
not intentional

**inequality**
state of being unequal

**mantle**
responsibility

**mentor**
a trusted advisor

**prejudice**
disadvantage due to judgement or action of another person

**reproduction**
the process of having babies

**sexualised**
given a sexual (relating to sex) character

**sheer**
complete; utter

**spectrum**
a range of something (e.g. opinions, feelings)

**statistically**
based on statistics (numerical facts)

**stereotype**
standard idea or model

**submissive**
inclined to submit (be obedient)

**synonymous**
having the same meaning

**tangible**
real; not imaginary

**triumph**
to win

*Emma Watson: Feminism*

ISBN: 978-1-76020-155-5

Introduction text copyright © 2016 Blake Publishing

Published by Blake Education Pty Ltd
ABN 50 074 266 023
Locked Bag 2022
Glebe NSW 2037
Ph: (02) 8585 4085
Fax: (02) 8585 4058
Email: info@blake.com.au
Web: www.blake.com.au

Introduction by Mark Stafford
Publisher: Katy Pike
Series Editor: Mark Stafford
Design and layout by The Modern Art Production Group
Printed by Thumbprints Utd